ILLUSTRATED

MAHABHARATHA

For Children

Retold in simple language with multi-coloured illustrations for young children

Vasan Publications

CONTENTS

Vasan Publications

25, Vasan Towers, Dr. T.C.M. Royan Road, Bangalore-560 053

Ph: 080-2670 5679/2670 5107,

Illustrations by : Chandu

www.mastermindbooks.com

ISBN 978-81-8468-243-4

BHISHMA'S VOW

This is not a recent story. It is a very ancient story which happened thousands of years ago.

Shantanu was the king of Hastinapur. He was wise, kind and just. All his citizens loved him and respected him. The river goddess Ganga was Shantanu's first wife. Shantanu had met Ganga at the river bank, fallen in love with her and proposed marriage to her. But then, Ganga had laid down certain conditions to say 'yes' to his proposal and had warned him that whatever she did, he was not to counter-question her. So desperate was the king to marry her that without a moment's hesitation, he had agreed to obey her conditions.

Ganga was a beautiful woman. She was also a devout wife and looked after the king with love and affection. They were so happy that Shantanu even forgot that a year had already passed. Meanwhile

Ganga gave birth to a baby boy. The king's happiness knew no bounds as he fondly looked at his heir. But his joy was short-lived. The same night Ganga carried the baby and headed towards the river. Shantanu was perplexed. So he followed her. By the time he could realise her intentions she had thrown the baby into the river. Shantanu was about to ask her the reason for her abnormal action when he remembered his promise to her at the time of their marriage. He could not question her about anything. Both of them returned to the palace silently.

Even after this incident, Shantanu's love for Ganga did not diminish in any way. But he was perplexed about her behaviour. How could she kill her own child? Was she a demon or a human, he wondered. Nevertheless, he decided to forget about this incident and continued to lead a happy life with Ganga. Subsequently, Ganga gave birth to another baby boy. The second baby also met the same fate as the first born and Shantanu turned pale with worry. But still, he did not have the courage to question Ganga. He felt very sad and depressed.

Ganga gave birth to five more baby boys, year after year. But all the babies were thrown into the river a few hours after their birth. And it was none other than their own mother who killed them.

When Ganga gave birth to a baby boy for the eighth time, Shantanu

could no longer bear the agony. By then, he had become a dejected man. When Ganga was about to throw the newborn into the river, Shantanu stopped her and asked her, "Do you know what you are doing? Are you a human or a devil? You have killed our seven sons. I can no longer bear it. I want to save atleast this child." He could not control his emotions.

Ganga smiled at his reaction and told "Oh, king Shantanu, I am neither a devil nor a human. I am the goddess Ganga Devi cursed for my faults. Now my curse is completed and I have to go back". Shantanu loved Ganga very much. He begged and pleaded with her not to desert him. But Ganga told the king that she had to return to her abode as she had fulfilled her task upon the earth. She then explained to Shantanu what her task was.

Long ago, there were eight demi-gods known as Ashta Vasus. Once, out of sheer greed, they wanted to steal Sage Vashista's divine cow and the youngest of them, by name Prabhasa stole the cow. Vashista was enraged at this and cursed them to be born as human beings upon the earth. When the Vasus sought to be forgiven, the sage relented and laid down that the seven Vasus could live only for a few hours upon the earth but, Prabhasa was to live his entire life upon the earth. These Ashta Vasus were the babies born to Ganga. The seven Vasus were thrown into the river and Prabhasa was the only survivor.

Ganga narrated this episode to Shantanu and disappeared after promising him that she would hand over Prabhasa to his care subsequently.

Seven years later, Shantanu witnessed a young lad practising archery by the river side. A strong feeling attracted him towards the boy. At that moment, Ganga appeared before the king and told him, "Here is your son Devavrat; He is not an ordinary person. He will earn fame as a great man. Look after him well". She then returned to her abode.

Shantanu was immensely happy and hugged the child. His heart swelled with love and affection. He took the boy to the palace and reared him well.

Devavrat grew up to be a brave and courageous boy. Shantanu had appointed a master for him. Devavrat thirsted for knowledge and excelled himself in all fields of education. As a true Kshatriya, he also perfected warfare and was hailed as the mightiest of all. Truthful and honest, he gained the respect of one and all. At the opportune time, Shantanu crowned Devavrat as the heir-prince.

In the meanwhile, Shantanu had gone on a hunt and near the river saw an extremely beautiful girl. She was the daughter of Dasaraja, a fisherman. Shantanu fell in love with her and sent a messenger to her father asking her hand in marriage.

"I am prepared to have my daughter wed the king" said Dasaraja, "But I have a condition" he added, "I want my daughter to be the queen and the child born to her to be the future king. If your king doesn't agree to this, ask him to forget about marrying my daughter".

Shantanu was worried. He found it impossible to live without Satyavati, Dasaraja's daughter. But how could he marry her? For he had already crowned Devavrat as the heir to the throne. There were none to equal Devavrat for the throne. So, Shantanu decided not to accept the condition laid down by Dasaraja. But he felt very depressed about losing Satyavati.

Devavrat knew his father's state of mind. So he met Dasaraja and pleaded with him to get Satyavati married to the king. Dasaraja was adamant. "Are you prepared to give up the throne for the sake of your father's happiness?" he asked.

Devavrat did not hesitate. "If it can bring happiness to my father, I do not want the throne. I am prepared to give it up. I swear", he said. But Dasaraja was not convinced. He asked Devavrat,

"O! Devavrat, it is easy for you to say that you do not want the throne. But you will get married and have children. Later on, your children will also have children. And if they claim their right to the throne, what will be the fate of Satyavati's children?"

Devavrat agreed with Dasaraja's thinking. He felt that it was a fair question. He thought for a while and said "Respected Sir, have no doubts about this. I hereby swear that I will be a bachelor throughout my life. I will never get married."

This decision by young Devavrat to lead his life all alone for the sake of his father's happiness drew appreciation from all the Suras. This vow came to be known as 'Bhishma's Vow'. Devavrat was hence forth called as Bhishma.

Devavrat returned to the palace and made arrangements for the marriage of Satyavati to his father. In the presence of hundreds of citizens, he again proclaimed that he was giving up his rights to the throne. Highly pleased with his son's sacrifice, Shantanu embraced Bhishma and blessed him as *"Iccha Marani*"*. "Let not death near you as long as you want it", he wished.

Bhishma is remembered through the ages as a great son of India.

**Iccha Marani :- One who could die only when and if he desired to die.*

AMBA'S REVENGE

Shantanu married Satyavati and led a happy life. Subsequently Satyavati gave birth to two sons. The eldest was Chitrangadh. After the demise of Shantanu, Bhishma crowned Chitrangadh as the king. But the king died shortly thereafter. So Bhishma coronated Vichitravirya, the second son, as the king. But since the boy was still young, Bhishma ruled the land on his behalf. There was peace and prosperity everywhere. Several years passed. Vichitravirya was now a young man and was of marriageable age.

The king of Kashi had three daughters by the names of Amba, Ambika and Ambalika, who were renowned for their beauty. A duel was arranged and the king proclaimed that he would give his daughters in marriage to the winner of this duel. Bhishma heard about this and set forth to Kashi. He defeated all the other princes and left for Hastinapur along with the three princesses. On the way Salvaraj challenged him to a war because he wanted to marry Amba. But Bhishma defeated him and reached Hastinapur.

Actually, Bhishma had selected these princesses as brides for Vichitravirya. But Amba wanted to marry Salvaraj and requested him to send her to Salvaraj.

On hearing this, Bhishma did not want to force her into an unwilling marriage with Vichitravirya. So he sent her back to Salvaraj. But Salvaraj was not prepared to accept her. "You can live with whoever carried you away", he scorned. He had not forgotten his humiliation at the hands of Bhishma. Amba returned to Hastinapur with a heavy heart. Bhishma felt sorry for her. By then, Vichitravirya had also decided not to marry Amba. She could not bear the humiliation. So she pleaded with Bhishma to marry her. But how could he? Had'nt he taken a vow not to marry? He said 'no' to her.

This infuriated Amba. She held Bhishma totally responsible for her plight. Hatred and revenge filled her thoughts. She sought the help of other kings to wage a war against Bhishma but none supported her. Her anger against Bhishma grew stronger. In desperation, she observed a very strict penance, praying to Lord Shiva. Her sole purpose was to kill Bhishma out of her own hands.

Pleased with Amba's penance, Shiva appeared before her. But the boon she wanted was against the divine spirit. "Bhishma has the blessings of all gods and goddesses", said Shiva, "Hence, nobody can kill him. But all humans on this earth are bound to

die sooner or later. You can kill Bhishma; but not now. You can do so in your next birth upon this earth. You will be born as a son to Drupad, the king of Panchala. Your wish will then be fulfilled."

Amba had only one aim in life-- to kill Bhishma. She was prepared to wait until even her next birth. She therefore headed straight to Drupad's palace and jumped into the sacrificial fire (yagna) being conducted there. Her body was reduced to ashes.

Amba was born as Drupad's son and was named Shikhandi; and waited for an opportunity to seek vengeance on Bhishma.

THE PANDAVAS & THE KAURAVAS

Vichitravirya had two sons. The eldest was Dhritarashtra, born blind. Hence Bhishma crowned the second son Pandu as the king. Pandu was a very capable king and ruled the land well.

Vichitravirya had a son by name Vidura through a chamber maid. Vidura was an able statesman and a scholar. He acted as an advisor to Pandu. Bhishma was the father figure to all of them.

Kunthi, daughter of the king of Mathura was Pandu's wife. Prior to her marriage, Durvasa a sage had taught her some Manthras. He had indicated to her that by chanting these, Kunthi could summon any celestial god and beget a son from him. Just to test the veracity of this, the young Kunthi invited Surya, the Sun God and got a son from him. But being a virgin and not married, she feared social outcry against her and placed the baby, which had been born with a pair of brilliant ear ornaments in a wooden box and gently pushed it into the river. Floating on the river, the box reached the hands of a childless charioteer. He handed the baby to his wife Radha. The couple named the boy as Karna because of his ear-ornaments and brought him up with love and affection.

According to a royal custom, Pandu took another wife Madri. But because of a curse, he could not get any child. Seeing his

plight, Kunthi confided in him about the mantras taught to her. So, he urged her and Madri to use these chants. With the result, Kunthi had three sons born of gods - Dharmaraj from Yama, Bhima from Vayu, the wind god and Arjun from Devendra. Madri gave birth to two sons Nakul and Sahadev from Ashwini Gods. These five sons of Pandu were the Pandavas. All of them were handsome, noble and courageous.

Because of his curse, Pandu had given up his kingdom and was living in the forest. He did not live for long. He died when the Pandavas were still youngsters. Entreating Kunthi to be a mother to all the five sons of Pandu, Madri burnt herself on the funeral pyre of her husband. On hearing about the death of Pandu and Madri, Bhishma and Vidur hastened to the forest and brought Kunthi and the Pandavas to Hastinapur.

Dhritarashtra had one hundred sons by the name of Kauravas. His wife was Gandhari. The eldest of the Kauravas was Duryodhana who, from a very young age, had nursed a deep hatred for the Pandavas; that is why he could not tolerate the Pandavas in Hastinapur. Pretending to be friendly with them, he plotted devious means of getting rid of them from the kingdom.

GURUKUL - THE SCHOOL

It is very important for the Kshatriyas—that is the warrior clan to be proficient in archery, fencing and other warfare. We already know that the Pandavas and the Kauravas were being brought up together by Bhishma. He always showed keen interest in their education and proficiency in warfare. He therefore wanted the best among the tutors to train Pandavas and Kauravas in archery and sword fighting.

One day all the princes were playing the ball game together and the ball fell into a dilapidated well. How to take out the ball was their problem. Just at that time, they spotted a brahmin. He was a thin person but his bright eyes and the glow on his face indicated a brilliant man. The brahmin listened to the children and said in a teasing voice, "You are from a warrior race and still you do not know how to take out the ball from the well!" The children were surprised. What is the relationship between the ball and the warrior race, they wondered. They raised this doubt with the brahmin. He replied, "Let me show you".

The brahmin was not an ordinary person. He pulled out a blade of grass and after chanting a mantra, threw it into the well. The grass hit the water with a lot of force and the ball bounced out of the well. The princes realised that he was an extraordinary man. They wanted to

know his name. But the brahmin smiled and said, “Go to your grandfather Bhishma, and narrate this incident to him. He will know who I am”.

It didn’t take long for Bhishma to know the identity of this brahmin. He was none other than Dronacharya. Bhishma had known that no one could match Drona’s skill in archery in the entire land of Bharat. So Bhishma hastened to meet Dronacharya and appointed him as the tutor for the princes. All the princes felt happy and proud that they were Dronacharya’s disciples.

Among all the princes, Arjun was Dronacharya’s favourite disciple. Arjun always aimed his bow very well. He always respected his Guru. And though the other princes received good training from their master, it was Arjun who excelled himself in archery.

Previously Drona had a friend by name Drupad. They were fellow students under Bharadhwaja. Drupad, the prince of Panchala had promised Drona that in proof of their true friendship, he would share his kingdom with Drona when he ascended the throne.

After completing his education, Drona married Kripacharya’s

sister. A son was born to the couple and he was named as Ashwathama. To ensure a good life for his son, Drona decided to seek employment under a king. He then remembered Drupada and also recalled his promise about sharing the kingdom. But when he went to meet Drupada a rude shock awaited him. Drupada refused to recognise him. "I do not know who you are", he said, "People will laugh if you say you are a friend of mine because you are a beggar and I am the king". Drona, a great scholar and a great warrior felt very humiliated. He did not want to stay there even for a moment. He went straight to Kripacharya and poured out all his anguish to him.

Ever since this incident, Drona waited for an opportunity to teach a lesson to the arrogant Drupada. With brave Arjun, with Duryodhan who was good at the mace, with the powerful Bhima and with courageous Yudhishtira as students, Drona felt that the time was right for him to seek his revenge against Drupada. So, first of all, he ordered Duryodhana to wage a war against the Panchala king and drag him by the hair through the battle field. But Duryodhana was no match for Drupad and was easily defeated by him. Disappointed Drona entrusted this task to Arjun. It did not take long for Arjun to defeat Drupad. He imprisoned the king and produced him before Drona. Drupad felt punished. All the insults that he had heaped on Drona flashed through his mind. He stood before Drona with a bowed head.

Since Drupad was defeated in the war, Drona had the right to claim the entire kingdom, as his own. But he was an unselfish person. So he told Drupad, "My friend, let one half of the kingdom be with you. I will retain the other half so that both of us can be equals. Then you will have no hesitation in accepting me as your friend."

This generous attitude of Drona made Drupada feel all the more humiliated. But instead of being grateful to him, a feeling of revenge grew strong in Drupad. He craved for a son who would be able to kill Drona.

DURYODHANA'S PLOT

Right from the day the Pandavas entered Hastinapur, the Kauravas and especially Duryodhan disliked them intensely. He was also extremely jealous of the Pandavas for they had earned the love and respect of the entire kingdom. By some means or the other, he wanted to kill the Pandavas, especially Bhima. But Duryodhana was fully aware that it would not be possible to kill Bhima through a wrestling match or with the mace. So Duryodhana had a sinister plot in mind.

One day, Duryodhana invited the Pandavas for a holiday by the riverside. How could the Pandavas know Duryodhana's devious mind? Thinking about all the enjoyment, they readily agreed. And what a lot of fun it was with horse-riding, boating, camp fire etc! On the last day, Duryodhana had arranged for a royal feast. Bhima, who was a glutton could not resist the many mouth-watering delicacies and sweet dishes. Happily, he ate greedily without knowing that a deadly poison had been mixed with his food.

In the night when the others were fast asleep, the Kauravas tied the hands and legs of Bhima and threw him into the river.

The next morning Yudhishtira found Bhima missing from his bed. Presuming that he had loitered away, the other Pandavas returned to the palace along with Kauravas.

Bhima who had sunk to the bottom of the river had lost consciousness but was not dead. Seeing his inert body on the river bed, the king of Nagalok treated him against the poison. The king knew of Duryodhana's evil intentions and hence warned Bhima to be careful about Duryodhana and his brothers. He gave him special food for extra-ordinary strength. Bhima thanked the residents of Nagalok for their hospitality and returned to Hastinapur.

Dharmaraj, Kunthi and the other Pandavas who were immensely worried about Bhima's strange disappearance were very happy to see him back. But not Duryodhana. He was baffled that Bhima had survived such a strong poison. This incident made Duryodhana all the more determined to kill the Pandavas as he knew that they were the rightful heirs to the throne of Hastinapur.

Having known about Duryodhana's hatred and jealousy, Bhima warned his brothers and mother about the danger posed by the Kauravas.

It was under these circumstances that Duryodhana met Karna.

EKALAVYA'S SACRIFICE

Hiranyadhanu was the king of Nishada. Hunting was the main occupation of his people. They were tribals. Ekalavya was the only son of Hiranyadhanu. It was his ardent desire to learn the art of archery from Dronacharya. So, one day he travelled to Hastinapur and witnessed Drona teaching the Pandavas and the Kauravas the art of archery. Ekalavya went straight to Drona and requested him to include him among his disciples. Drona questioned Ekalavya about his caste and creed. And he turned down the request on the ground that he taught only the Kshatriyas. Disappointed Ekalavya returned to the forest. He then made a statue of Drona in mud and installed it at the place where he usually practised archery. Everyday he prostrated before the statue and practised archery. His concentration was so high that he could gain mastery over archery. He acquired immense knowledge about it also.

One day, Drona took his pupils to the forest to teach them hunting. It was the same forest where Ekalavya practised archery. Inside the forest Drona observed bow marks on the tree barks indicating archery practice. Just then, a hound standing near Drona started barking. Within a moment the hound's mouth was covered

by seven arrows. Drona was astonished to find that someone had used his bow in the right direction and the exact place just by listening to the barking sound. Drona was therefore very curious to know more about this archer who had excelled his own disciples.

Arjun, who was standing next to Drona was baffled. ' I will ensure that none can equal you in archery' Drona had promised Arjuna. 'But was he teaching someone else secretly wondered Arjun.

Both Drona and Arjun went in search of the archer. They saw Ekalavya who recognised Dronacharya. Ekalavya was delighted. He felt as if he had found a treasure and putting down the bow, prostrated before his Guru. Drona was immensely pleased. He asked Ekalavya "Son! you are an excellent archer. Who is your Guru?"

His guru was right in front of him. But instead, Ekalavya took Drona to the statue and said, "Sir, my Guru is none other than yourself, an expert archer and an unparalleled warrior. I have prepared your statue out of mud and imagining your physical presence, I practice archery", replied Ekalavya in a humble voice.

Drona then recalled Ekalavya's earlier request to teach him archery. He instructed the boy to exhibit his talent. Ekalavya obeyed his instructions and demonstrated his skill with the bow and the arrow. All the princes present there were astonished with his skill.

Drona too could not believe his own eyes. He admired the great achievement by a tribal but could not forget his promise to Arjuna. He called Ekalavya to come nearer and said, "Son! Since you say that you learnt it from me, shouldn't you pay me my Gurudakshina?"

Ekalavya in reply said "Sir, I am at your bidding. Whatever you want, I will give it to you".

Drona was bound by his promise to Arjuna and wanted to impair Ekalavya's capability to use the bow and the arrow. This would remove any challenges to Arjun's supremacy in archery. He therefore said, "Ekalavya, cut your right thumb and offer it to me as your fee".

Ekalavya realised Drona's intentions, but without any hesitation, he chopped off his right thumb and willingly offered it to Drona.

Drona was immensely pleased with Ekalavya's devotion and after complimenting him about this, returned to the palace along with his disciples.

KARNA - DURYODHANA

Whenever people talk about friendship, they always bring up Karna and Duryodhana's names. For, they had a very strong bond of friendship between them.

Drona had taught the princes everything about warfare. He had also told them about the methods to be followed during a war. He had explained about the right and the wrong, the do's and don'ts a Kshatriya should follow. Arjun attained excellence in archery

under Drona's training. Dharmaraja was adept at fighting from a chariot. Bhima and Duryodhana acquired mastery in using the mace. Nakul and Sahadev were good as horse-riders.

Drona wanted the entire Hastinapur to know about the expertise of the princes in waging wars. So he made suitable arrangements for such a show of games.

On the appointed day, the citizens of Hastinapur flocked to the arena of war sports. For, they had an opportunity to watch the princes demonstrate individually, their skill and knowledge, and compete with each other.

Dhritharashtra, Gandhari, Kunthi, Vidura, Bhishma, Kripa and Drona were seated on the dais. The commoners were also provided with seats. The entire Hastinapur wore a festive look.

Shortly, all the princes, that is, Dharmaraja with his four brothers and Duryodhana accompanied by his ninety-nine brothers entered the arena. They were all dressed in a war-like fashion and were armed suitably.

The competition began after the Vedic chant by the Raj Purohit. Conches were sounded and drums were beaten to indicate the commencement of the games. It was then announced that the princes should exhibit their capabilities. The archers, the fencers and the wrestlers amongst the princes demonstrated their talents. "Bravo! Bravo" shouted the excited crowd. Bhima and Duryodhana's deftness in using the mace also delighted the crowd. Nakul, Sahadev and the other Kauravas also drew appreciation from the spectators.

It was now Arjun's turn. Partha (Arjun) was Drona's prize student. When he entered the arena, the spectators clapped their hands and cried out "Hail Arjun! Hail Arjun!". Arjun, the warrior, demonstrated before the public all that he had learned from his teacher. The crowd applauded each and every feat of Arjun. Kunthi felt very happy and proud of him.

The only person who could not tolerate this adulation towards Arjun was Duryodhan. He felt restless and agitated that none of his younger brothers could excel Arjun. If he were to score victory over the Pandavas, he ought to have a very able person who could defeat Arjun. Otherwise his ambition to rule Hasthinapur would be shattered - thus thought Duryodhan.

Suddenly a man stood up from amongst the spectators and entering the arena proclaimed that he too would like to demonstrate his skill as a warrior and that he could prove himself to be far better than Arjun.

Drona was annoyed that a stranger trespassed into the arena which was meant only for the princes. He was all the more angry that this stranger had ridiculed Arjun. But Arjun accepted this challenge from a newcomer and Drona had no other option but to give permission. But he was curious to know more about this person whose face radiated an inner strength. He had a pair of earrings which dazzled in the sunlight. He was Karna!

These dazzling earrings also caught the attention of Kunthi and it immediately dawned on her that this was her eldest born. She was filled with anguish to see her two children facing each other in a challenge.

When Karna displayed all the feats of Arjun effortlessly, Duryodhana was delighted. “Finally, I have found someone who can combat with Arjun”, he rejoiced. He immediately went to Karna and embracing him said, “From now on, you are my brother”.

The contest between Arjun and Karna created a lot of excitement amongst the spectators. They knew that this would be a very significant contest, for both Arjun and Karna were great warriors.

Kunthi, the mother of both Karna and Arjun just couldn’t witness the scene. She knew for certain that Karna was the child she had set adrift in the river long ago. Moreover, at close quarters one could make out a striking resemblance between the two brothers. Thinking about the outcome, she fainted.

Suddenly an idea occurred to Drona. He decided that he would allow only princes to take part in this contest. He immediately conveyed this suggestion to Kripa. Kripa at once entered the arena and told Arjun, “Arjun! Dronacharya has agreed to this combat. But prior to this, both of you have to proclaim about yourselves”.

Arjun had no difficulty in proclaiming about his royal origin. It was now Karna’s turn to reply. The warrior told the spectators that his name was Karna. But what next? He did not know who his real parents were, what his clan was, or any other information about himself. Red in the face, Karna felt distressed that fate had cheated him. He felt utterly humiliated. Kripa took advantage of this opportunity and spoke again.

“You do not know who you are. You are just an ordinary soldier. So, you do not qualify yourself to take part in a contest meant only for the royal blood. You may leave the arena ,” he said in an insulting tone.

Drona and Kripa did not have any grudge against Karna. But fearful of Arjuna's defeat by this warrior, they had to prevent Karna's participation in the contest.

Karna could not say anything. He did not know who he was, except that he had been brought up by a charioteer. He had no status in the society.

Duryodhana did not like Karna being humiliated in such a fashion. He desperately needed someone to fight against Arjun. So, he quickly ran upto Karna and said, "I am the prince of Hastinapur and upon my authority, I am appointing you as the king of Anga. You are now a king. So, I dare anyone to say anything against you". So saying he placed a crown on Karna's head. He also performed all the necessary rites to bestow the kingdom of Anga on Karna.

Bhishma, Drona and Vidura were speechless. The Pandavas found Duryodhana's behaviour very strange. Bhima thought it to be ridiculous. He roared with laughter and said "A charioteer's son! King of Anga! Ho... Ho..."

But Duryodhana ignored them all and hugging Karna in a friendly way drove away in his chariot.

The contest ended and the crowd dispersed. Some praised Arjun, others Karna but none knew that Karna was the eldest among Kunthi's children.

From that day onwards Duryodhana and Karna became very close friends and Karna remained loyal to his friend till the very last.

Karna was a great warrior and a good human being. But his only drawback was that he did not know about his origin. He had learnt archery under Parashurama by representing to him that he was a brahmin. This was because Parashurama hated Kshatriyas and had vowed not to teach anyone of them. Karna became a favourite student of Parashurama and learnt from him the usage of a master weapon known as Brahmastra.

One day Parashurama was taking his afternoon nap reclining on Karna's lap, when a bee bit Karna's thigh. Blood started flowing but since Karna did not want to disturb his Guru's sleep, he bore the pain without flinching. When the blood oozed to Parashurama's

cheek, he woke up. Karna tried to explain his action to his Guru but Parasurama was not convinced. He did not believe that a brahmin could with stand that much physical pain. Angered that Karna had told him a lie about being a brahmin he cursed his student. "Karna! You have deceived me by uttering a lie. I hereby curse you that whatever you have learnt from me shall fail you when you need it most".

Karna was aghast. All his dedication had become futile. He fell at his Guru's feet. "Please forgive me", he pleaded, "In my determination to seek knowledge from you, I lied about my being a brahmin". But Parasurama did not relent. "Karna, you have been one of my best students. But I am punishing you for your lie. You may remain a great warrior. But you will be unable to recall the Brahmastra when you need it most." Karna was disappointed and left the school.

Karna was reputed for charity and generosity. To test him, Indra once put on the garb of an old man and begged Karna for his ear-rings and armour. Karna donated these without any hesitation. Pleased with his generosity, Indra revealed himself and bade him to ask for any boon. "I ask for your weapon, the Shaktya", Karna replied and got it in return. It was a very powerful weapon and had never failed to destroy anything that it touched.

THE WAX MANSION

Pandavas' courage and the love and affection people showered on them created a deep jealousy within Duryodhana. His thoughts were always about killing the Pandavas. His plot to poison Bhima had failed. So, he wanted a good plan to wipe them out totally. His brothers aided him in his actions. Dhritharashtra adored his eldest son Duryodhana and could not bring himself to rebuke and correct his son though he knew of Duryodhana's evil intentions.

Duryodhana's mother Gandhari also doted on her eldest son and thus Duryodhana fully exploited the love of his parents for his selfishness.

Duryodhana once came to know that a grand festival was being arranged in Varanavati and he decided to use the occasion to achieve his aim. So, he paid a visit to the Pandavas and praising the beauty of Varanavati, he described the great festival to be conducted there with all the pomp and grandeur. He also told them that the people of the city were eagerly awaiting the Pandavas to grace the occasion. The unsuspecting Pandavas agreed to go, more so, since Dhrithrashtra also told them to witness the festival.

Overjoyed that Pandavas had agreed to go to Varanavati, Duryodhana had a palatial mansion built for their stay. It was made of wax and other inflammable material like jute, dry grass, etc. The idea was to set the mansion on fire at night when the Pandavas were fast asleep and make people believe that it was a fire accident. No one would suspect the Kauravas.

The Pandavas came to know of this wax house through Vidura. They felt deeply hurt that their own kith and kin were betraying them. But pretending to be unaware of the danger to their lives, the Pandavas proceeded to Varanavati but tried to find out if there was any escape route from the wax mansion. Luckily for them, Vidura had engaged an expert miner who had dug a tunnel under a chamber leading to a pit in the forest.

Duryodhana had employed many servants to keep a watch over the Pandavas. Kunthi was also staying with her children in the mansion. The Pandavas, familiarized themselves thoroughly with the tunnel route, somehow or the other, escaping the attention of the guards.

Within a few days, Vidura sent a secret word to the Pandavas informing them about the precise day on which the mansion was to be set on fire. That night, Kunthi prepared a sumptuous feast for all the servants. Soon after feast all the servants were fast asleep. Shortly afterwards, the Pandavas themselves set fire to the mansion. Soon the entire building was ablaze but not before the Pandavas made good their escape. Seeing the fire, people rushed to the spot. By that time, the building had been reduced to ashes. Believing the Pandavas to be dead, these people conveyed the news to Hastinapur. But then, the dead bodies charred inside the mansion were not those of the Pandavas. They were of the servants.

Duryodhana was absolutely delighted to hear that Pandavas died in the fire. But outwardly he put on a sad face and pretended to grieve over their death.

With utmost difficulty, the Pandavas crossed through the tunnel and entered the dense forest. With the exception of the powerful Bhima, all the others were exhausted. So he carried them through the forest and reached the Ganges where Vidura had arranged for a boat for them. They crossed the river in total darkness and entered another mighty forest. From there, the Pandavas marched on, eating the forest produce and sleeping by turns. They were ever vigilant and ever confident that justice would be theirs sooner or later.

Hidimba, a demoness, ruled over the forest where Pandavas had sought refuge. One day, while Bhima was fetching some water for his mother and brothers, Hidimba saw him and wanted to marry him. She herself proposed marriage to Bhima. But he was a human and she, a demoness. So, Hidimba's brother Hidimb objected to this marriage and challenged Bhima to a fight. Bhima lifted up the demon with his powerful arms and killed him by thrashing him on the ground. He then took Hidimba to Kunthi. Kunthi agreed to this marriage and so, Bhima and Hidimba were married. Hidimba looked after the Pandavas well. She cooked them good food and took care to see that they came to no harm in the forest. Subsequently she became pregnant. Bhima was very happy.

Meanwhile, the Pandavas reached the city of Ekachakra. But Hidimba did not agree to go with them for she said "I cannot bear to live outside the forest." Shortly afterwards, she gave birth to a son called Ghatotkacha.

In the city of Ekachakra, the Pandavas lived in the guise of brahmins, begging for their food. They brought home such food and Kunthi always divided it into two portions - one portion for Bhima alone and the other portion for the rest of them. None could imagine or recognise them as the princes of Hastinapur!

One day, Kunthi heard her neighbour's wife cry. So she went to their house to find out the reason for such anguish. The neighbour's wife, with tears rolling down her cheeks said, "O! Great lady! You have been like a mother to us. But I do not know how you can help us, because, this relates to a wicked Rakshasa by name Bakasura. Earlier, he used to pounce upon people and after killing them indiscriminately, would eat human flesh. To prevent such slaughter, the citizens of Ekachakra agreed to send a human being to the demon daily, along with a cartload of rice and other delicacies. Tomorrow is my turn and so, I have to send my only son to Bakasura. Only God can help us."

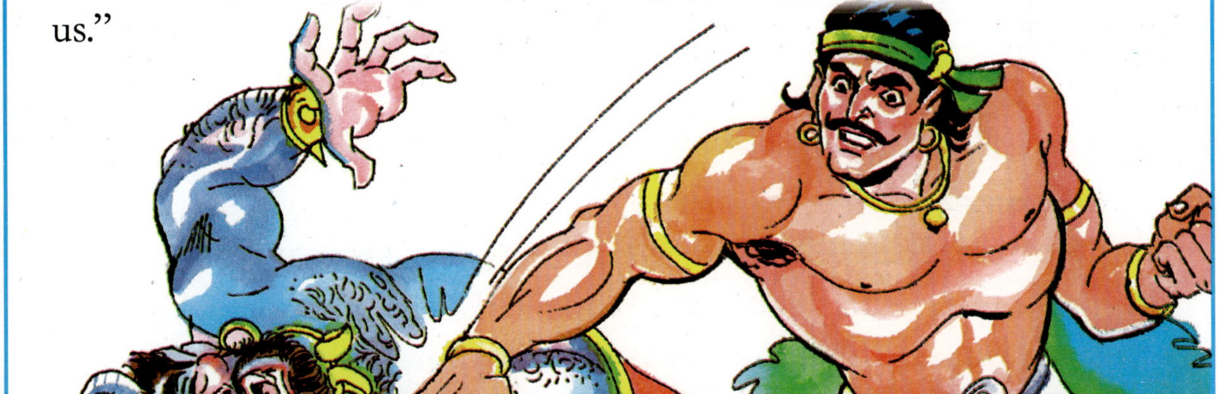

Kunthi pacified the woman and told her, "Don't worry, I will send one of my sons in place of your son".

Bhima immediately agreed to go to Bakasura as his food. His aim was to kill the Rakshasa and provide peaceful living to the people of the city.

The next day Bhima drove the cart loaded with rice and other food straight to the demon's cave. But even before he reached the cave, unable to bear his hunger, Bhima himself ate up all the food in the cart and gave out loud belch. On hearing this, the demon, already angry that his food had been delayed, rushed out of his cave only to find that the cart was empty. He charged towards Bhima to eat him up. Bhima just raised his fist and gave a severe blow to the demon. Then ensued a big fight between them but finally, Bhima threw him down and smashed him to death. The Rakshasa howled so loudly in pain that hearing this, the people of the city trembled with fear, not knowing the outcome of this fight. But soon, their fear turned into joy when they saw Bhima dragging the body of the dead Bakasura. Little did they realise that this courageous man was none other than Bhima, one of the Pandava princes.

DRAUPADI'S SWAYAMVAR

Draupadi was the daughter of Drupad, king of Panchala. Dhristadyumna was her brother. Drupad who had once been defeated by Arjun decided that a great warrior like him would be the best match for Draupadi. Drupad had earlier believed the Pandavas to be dead but had also heard rumours that they had escaped from the wax house. So, he hoped that Arjun would attend the Swayamvar.

Draupadi's Swayamvar had been arranged in the city of Kampilya. Many princes had often dreamt about marrying this world renowned beautiful princess. News of the Swayamvar also reached the Pandavas. They decided to witness the Swayamvar along with the brahmins going in groups to Kampilya.

The entire city of Kampilya had been decorated for the occasion with arches and festoons. Houses were painted. There was a joyous and festive atmosphere. People put on their best clothes and excitedly talked about the royal wedding.

The marriage hall wore a magnificent look. In the midst of the hall a big platform had been built and a huge vessel of water was placed at the centre. Right above the vessel was a revolving disc with a fish hooked to it. The prince aspiring to marry Draupadi had to string his bow and with it, shoot an arrow to hit the eye of the fish and that too, by looking at its reflection in the water kept below.

Drupad had purposely set up such an extremely difficult test for the archer for he knew that only a hero like Arjun would be able to accomplish the feat.

Many valiant princes had gathered there to prove their skill and win the hand of Draupadi. Duryodhan, Karna, Jarasandha, the king of Magadh, Shishupala, Shalya and many, many more able kings and princes were there. The Pandavas stood in a corner amidst a group of Brahmins.

At the auspicious moment, Draupadi, looking all the more dazzling as a bride-to-be, entered the hall. All the suitors were anxious. "Will Draupadi be mine?" was their thought. But was it so easy? Didn't they have to win the contest?

The kings and princes rose one after the other to string the bow. Some couldn't even lift it. Even if they could, one look at the rapidly revolving disc made them cross-eyed. They all gave it up.

Then Karna stood up and walked towards the dais. But Draupadi denied him the chance saying that she could not possibly marry the son of a charioteer. Feeling small, Karna returned to his seat. Finally, it looked as if Draupadi's Swayamvar would not take place at all.

Amidst the murmur of disappointment stood up Arjun, seeking permission to contest. "How could a brahmin succeed

when valiant princes have failed?" ridiculed the Kshatriyas. But impressed by Arjun's noble look, Drupad gave him the permission to contest. Arjun was delighted. He stringed the bow and concentrating on the reflection of the fish in the water, he aimed his arrow. The arrow directly hit the eye of the fish.

While the brahmins and others shouted with joy and excitement, the defeated princes showed their anger on Drupada. "Why did you allow this? Can a princess of Draupadi's stature marry a poor brahmin?" was their ridicule. Some threatened to kill Drupad. Some protested loudly about being insulted. Amidst this confusion, Bhima and Yudhishtira were afraid that someone might recognise them. Meanwhile Draupadi with love shining in her eyes for the valiant Arjun, garlanded him. Lord Krishna and his brother Balaram who had also graced the occasion, pacified the princes. During the uproar Arjun and his brothers along with Draupadi quietly slipped out of the marriage hall. Seeing them departing, Drupad asked his son to follow them to know their true identity.

It was Arjun who had gained the hand of Draupadi and only he should have wed her. But destiny willed otherwise. The Pandavas returning to their abode, called out to their mother, "Mother, come and see our alms for to-day". And Kunthi also called out from inside the house, "Whatever you have got, please share it among yourselves." But when Kunthi actually saw Draupadi, the seriousness of what she said, struck her. But she extended a warm welcome to Draupadi.

Dhristadyumna who had followed the Pandavas, closely observed them and he was delighted at what he saw. He returned to his father and told him that the five brahmins were none other than the Pandavas and that Kunthi was also with them. Drupada promptly invited the Pandavas and Kunthi to Kampilya and on Kunthi's instructions, gave his daughter in marriage to all the five brothers. Lord Krishna and Balaram witnessed the marriage. Pandavas felt very happy at the outcome of events because

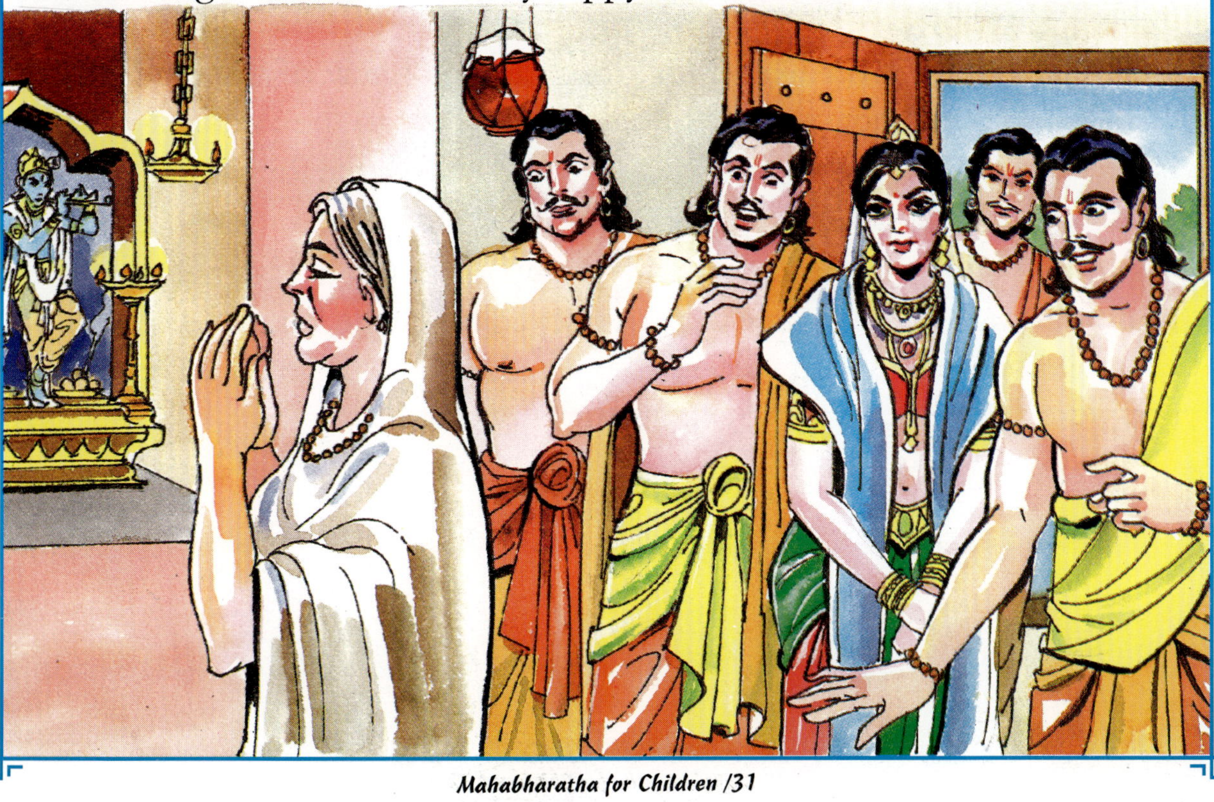

they had the support of Drupada and most important of all, Krishna, the universal protector was with them.

When news about Draupadi's Swayamvar reached Hastinapur, Duryodhana's hatred and jealousy knew no bounds. His bitter enemies, who, he thought, were burnt to ashes in Varanavati, were very much alive. To add to this, they were married to Draupadi and also gained the friendship of Drupad.

Duryodhana found the situation unbearable. When he consulted Karna, his friend advised him to wage a war against the Pandavas, a conduct befitting a warrior. Duryodhana after taking the consent of his blind father, broached the topic with Bhishma, Drona and other elders but they did not support him on this. Instead, they advised him, "Don't nurture any hatred towards your cousins. It will only demean you. You will also lose the good will of the people. So, treat the Pandavas well. After all, they have not done any injustice to you. Give them half the kingdom and end this enemity".

Neither Dhrithrashtra nor Duryodhana could go against the advice of Bhishma and Drona. So, reluctantly, they sent Vidura to the Pandavas to bring them back to Hastinapur.

Drupad had never liked Duryodhana. He knew of Duryodhana's plots to kill the Pandavas. He therefore objected to the Pandavas going back to Hastinapur but on Krishna's advice, agreed that they should claim their kingdom.

In the end, the Pandavas and Draupadi entered Hastinapur to a tumultous welcome. People were overjoyed to see the Pandavas alive and also to have them as their rulers. Only the Kauravas found it unpalatable and were biding their time to avenge the Pandavas.

THE RAJASUYA YAGNA

Dhrithrashtra totally ignored the Pandavas. He seemed to have forgotten that they were his brother's children. Their popularity and prosperity were unbearable to him. Hence, when he was forced into giving half the kingdom to the Pandavas, he deliberately allotted a barren and desolate land to them. Without grudging this offer, Yudhishtira accepted it and with his brothers, Draupadi and Kunthi, settled down in the place. Soon the Pandavas turned the barren land into a golden land. They built palaces and forts and also provided all the amenities fit for a great city. Thus a small place grew into a mighty capital called Indraprastha.

Soon, the people of the neighbouring places accepted Yudhishtira as their king and several kings also sought his patronage by offering monetary tributes. In no time Yudhishtira's coffers were full. He therefore wanted to expand his kingdom. After all, he had the support of his valiant brothers.

At that time Yudhishtira's friends suggested that he conduct the Rajasuya Yagna so that he could become the emperor of a vast kingdom. But since they had to ensure whether there were other kings who could

oppose him, Yudhishtira consulted his friend Krishna about this. Krishna told him that Magadha's king Jarasandha was the only king who was capable of challenging Yudhishtira's sovereignty. Hence, Jarasandha had to be defeated. Jarasandha was a wicked king. He had terrorized the entire world and Krishna wanted him to be annihilated. But Dharmaraja did not want to confront war with anybody. After devoting a lot of thought, Bhima, Krishna and Arjuna went in disguise to see Jarasandha's capital Girivraja.

Jarasandha was born as two halves of a body. A lady named Jara, out of her capability had enjoined the two parts so that it became a full baby and blessed him with immense power. Thus Jarasandha became very powerful. Krishna and the Pandavas in the guise of being brahmins, participated in the Yagna that was taking place in Girivraj. But, Jarasandha's sharp eye noticed some scars and immediately realised that these ought to be war scars. He even identified Bhima. When Jarasandha demanded the truth, Pandavas replied frankly that they had come to seek combat with him. Undaunted, Jarasandha invited Bhima for a fight again. without weapons. Bhima and Jarasandha were so strong that they fought for a fortnight without any signs of exhaustion. Even when Bhima managed to split Jarasandha's body into two halves, they would immediately adhere together and Lo! Jarasandha was ready for a fight again.

Not knowing what to do, Bhima looked at Krishna for guidance and he saw Krishna tearing a straw into half and throwing them in totally opposite directions. Bhima took the hint and he tore Jarasandha into two halves and threw them in opposite directions so far away from each other that they could not come back together. Thus, Jarasandha died and Pandavas were victorious.

Pandavas freed all the princes who were imprisoned by Jarasandha and crowned his son as the king of Magadha. Now Yudhishtira could proclaim himself as the emperor of the entire world.

Yudhishtira made hectic preparations for the Rajasuya Yagna. He invited many kings for the event. Duryodhana, Karna, Bhishma, Drona, Shakuni, the Prince of Gandhara, Sishupala, Krishna and several others accepted his invitation and reached Indraprastha to witness the Yagna.

On the ultimate day of the Yagna, Yudhishtira was to be proclaimed the emperor and a custom to render first honour to the guest who was considered most worthy among all others was to be followed. It was a huge congregation and Yudhishtira was of the opinion that Krishna should be honoured first.

Sishupala, the king of Chedi, hated Krishna and could not tolerate him. Laughing in derision he ridiculed Krishna of being a thief, of being the son of a cowherd and heaped many more insults on him.

Unable to tolerate Krishna being ridiculed, the elderly Bhishma stood up and revealed the secret behind Sishupala's birth.

Shishupala was Krishna's relative through his father Vasudeva. Shishupala was born ugly with three eyes and four arms and the royal astrologer had predicted that he would meet his death at the hands of the one who would cure him of his ugliness. Shishupala's mother roamed from town to town in search of a cure for her son's ugliness and in Dwarka, Krishna touched the baby and the baby turned out to be a normal looking one. But, she was grieved to think that her son would die at the hands of Krishna. Krishna consoled her by saying, "Dear Aunt! I can condone one hundred mistakes of Shishupala; If he exceeds this limit, he is bound to die".

Enraged at Bhishma, Shishupala turned his ire towards Krishna and ridiculed him further. Since his insults crossed the one hundred mark, Krishna stood up and used his Sudarshana Chakra towards Shishupala which chopped his head. He was thus slain.

Rajasuya Yagna was celebrated with a lot of pomp and pageantry and Yudhishtira was recognised as the emperor. The princes, priests, and other elders who had gathered for the occasion praised the magnificence

of the Yagna and returned to their places. Duryodhana burned with jealousy at the sight of Pandavas' prosperity. His jealousy knew no bounds when he saw the artistically built palace with its crystal floors so exquisitely designed that it was difficult to differentiate between a fountain of water and a crystal floor. Duryodhana was so lost in his jealousy and mistaking the floor, he slipped into water and fell down. Draupadi who witnessed this scene from her balcony burst into uncontrollable laughter. Duryodhana was enraged, to say the least. He was all the more determined to punish the Pandavas by driving them out of Indraprastha by hook or by crook.

THE GAMBLE

Shakuni was the prince of Gandhara. Gandhari was his sister. Thus, Shakuni was Duryodhana's maternal uncle and was his constant companion in Hastinapur.

Shakuni was fully aware of Pandava's might and also knew of Duryodhana's intense hatred towards them. The evil minded Shakuni nurtured this hatred and advised Duryodhana to destroy the Pandava brothers. After the incident at Indraprastha, Shakuni went to the forlorn Duryodhana and told him, "My dear nephew! I know a way to drive the Pandavas out of Indraprastha without any fight and without shedding any blood." Duryodhana's eyes lighted up in hope. He asked, "Uncle, how is it possible?". Shakuni replied, "Yudhishtira is very fond of the game of dice. You invite him for a game and I will play on your behalf. I will trick him into defeat and thus win his kingdom and his wealth for you. Do you like my plan?" Wouldn't Duryodhana be delighted at such an opportunity? But before sending a word to the Pandavas, Duryodhana and Shakuni went to Dhrithrashtra and explained their plan of inviting Yudhishtira for a game of dice, defeating him totally and taking away all his wealth and

kingdom from him. Dhrithrashtra at first did not favour the plan. But when Duryodhana insisted on this, Dhrithrashtra out of his blind love for his son relented. Ultimately, he summoned Vidura to invite Yudhishtira for the game of dice.

Yudhishtira had vowed that as an emperor he would never indulge in such games. But since his elderly uncle had summoned him, he went to Hastinapur alongwith his brothers and the royal retinue.

Duryodhana had a magnificient hall specially erected for the game. Many distinguished persons of the Kuru clan, royal teachers and officials were present in the hall on the day of the game and a huge platform had been erected. Shakuni invited Yudhishtira to the dais to start the game upon which Yudhishtira asked Duryodhana as to who would play with him. Duryodhana replied that his uncle Shakuni would cast the dice instead of him. Yudhishtira was confident of defeating Duryodhana in a game of dice but felt diffident against Shakuni as Shakuni was an expert player. So, he hesitated and said, "How

could Shakuni play on your behalf when it is you who have invited me to this game?" Duryodhana looking, deridingly asked, "Well! Are you afraid of losing to my uncle?" Yudhishtira flushed with embarrassment and said, "Duryodhana, I am not a coward, I shall play". The hall was full and everybody knew that the game would end in a bitter way, but they could do nothing about it. At first, gold, silver and ornaments were wagered and Yudhishtira lost them in no time. One by one he pledged his servants, his chariots, horses, armies and lost them too. The fervent plea made by his brothers to stop the game did not have any effect on Yudhishtira. When he had nothing more to pledge he staked Sahadev and Nakul and Shakuni's cunning game made him lose them too. Shakuni taunted him by saying, "Yudhishtira, after all they are your step brothers, and that is why you could stake them. I bet you wouldn't dare offer Bhima and Arjuna as stakes." Yudhishtira by that time was feeling thoroughly reckless and stung by Shakuni's retort continued the game by offering the ever victorious Arjun and Bhima as wagers. He lost them too. Shakuni then reminded Yudhishtira about Draupadi and said, "There is a very valuable jewel in your possession. I call upon you to continue the game with your wife Draupadi as wager". The desperate Yudhishtira pledged her too, and lost her. Duryodhana stood up in the assembly and shouted that he had won the Pandavas and Draupadi and they had to become his slaves. The entire gathering was stunned. Some wept with distress. Some blamed Duryodhana for the situation. Bhishma, Drona and Krupa were worried about the consequences.

Duryodhana roared like a lion, "Draupadi will henceforth be our maid. She is at our command". He turned towards Vidura and said, "Vidura! Go and fetch her." Vidura exclaimed "Have you become insane? You are heading towards your own destruction". Duryodhana ignored Vidura's caution and sent a charioteer to fetch Draupadi. He was intent on humiliating Draupadi in full view of the gathering. Draupadi refused to go to the court of Duryodhana and said "How could a man stake his wife after he himself had lost the game. When I do not belong

to him, how could he have the right to pledge me as a pawn? I refuse to come." Duryodhana was enraged on hearing this answer. "How dare the maid talks back like this? Duhshyasana, my brother! bring that maid here, even if you have to drag her by the hair. This is my order."

Duhshyasana was wicked. He went quickly to Draupadi's chamber, caught her by her long black hair and dragged her to the assembly. Draupadi was extremely angry. She argued that she could not be staked as a pawn as Yudhishtira had lost his freedom to stake her much earlier. She appealed to the elders like Bhishma, Drona, Kripa and Dhrithrashtra not to allow such a misdeed. Duryodhana had exceeded the limits of decency. Totally ignoring what was right and what was wrong, and also ignoring that the assembly consisted of male members and the elders, Duryodhana instructed Duhshyasana to sieze Draupadi's garments and disrobe her. The gathering was aghast. How could anybody tolerate a lady being thus insulted? Even Dhritarashtra had not anticipated that the matter would be carried out so far. He begged of his son, "Oh! my dear son, Do not resort to such acts and bring disrepute to the Kaurava clan", Bhishma and Drona were full of grief that they had to

witness such a scene. But, Duryodhana was adamant. He ordered his brother to pull out Draupadi's sari. The hapless Draupadi trembled with fear like a poor fawn stricken by a tiger. None among the gathering could protect her. Her five husbands who were described as the mighty ones were now Kaurava slaves. At that moment, she could only think of Divine Intervention and prayed to Lord Krishna to come to her help. As Duhshyasana tried to disrobe Draupadi's one saree, another garment would appear on her and soon a heap of garments were piled up in the assembly.

Duhshyasan went on pulling her garments and there seemed to be no end to them. He was so tired that he had to give up. While the assembly watched this miracle, the frustrated Duryodhana walked out of the assembly.

Draupadi slowly opened her eyes. The Pandavas stood in one corner bowing their heads in shame. It was Bhima who broke the deathly silence. He swore, "Sooner or later I shall rend the breast and drink the blood of Duhshyasana." Draupadi also swore that till Duhshyasana was killed, she would not tie up her hair. Nature also seemed to protest against such a shameful act. Suddenly the earth seemed to quiver. There were several evil omens. Rain also poured out of its fury.

Dhrithrashtra called Draupadi to his side and attempted to soothe her by saying, "Child, my son has erred. Whatever you want, I will grant to you as an atonement for his mistakes." Draupadi a devout wife, wanted her husbands to be freed from bondage, she also asked for return of the weapons. Dhrithrashtra was even prepared to give back Indraprastha to them. But, self respect would not make Draupadi to accept the kingdom from her enemies. She refused this offer.

The Pandavas left the cursed hall stunned by the turn of events. Draupadi followed them.

Duryodhana was extremely angry when he heard that his blind father had returned all the weapons to the Pandavas and freed them from bondage. He showed his anger on his father. The poor Dhrithrashtra did not even have the courage to stop his son's shouting. Finally, Duryodhana pressurised Dhrithrashtra to call Yudhishtira once again for the game of dice and that whoever was the loser was to go on exile to the forest for twelve years and spend the thirteenth year incognito. If they were recognised in the thirteenth year, they were to go into exile for another twelve years. The elders tried their level best to make Duryodhana come to his senses and not to bring any more misfortune to the Pandavas. How could Duryodhana agree when he didn't want them alive. His sole intention was to banish them forever.

Yudhishtira too could not resist the temptation of playing the game and win back what he had lost. So, he returned to Hastinapur and sat again for the game of dice. Needless to say, Yudhishtira lost again and had to leave for the forest.

When they set out for the forest, the citizens of Hastinapur requested them not to go. Their grief and lamentation filled the sky. When Dhrithrashtra learnt about their departure he was filled with even more fear and anxiety. But Duryodhana was not moved. Bhishma and Drona

could not even utter a word because they were under the obligation of Dhrithrashtra.

When Krishna came to know of the incident, he went to Hastinapur and took his sister Subhadra who was Arjuna's wife and her young son Abhimanyu to Dwarka. When Draupadi's brother Dhristadyumna heard of Draupadi's humiliation, he vowed to take revenge against the Kauravas. Kunthi stayed with Vidura.

THE EXILE

To be in exile in a forest is a very tough experience because a forest is full of wild animals. It is an area where Rakshasaas roam about freely. Mostly it is dark in the forest. One has to go in search of water and live on tubers and fruits. The Pandavas who had always lived in a royal style had to face all such hardships in the forest. But their courage and their righteousness never failed them.

Yudhishtira alongwith his brothers and wife lived in a forest called Kamyaka. Not many people lived there. Only a few sages could be found for living in a forest was really very tough. All such hardships constantly reminded them about Duryodhana's treachery. They could never forget that their hard-earned kingdom was lost to Duryodhana in a deceitful game nor could they forgive him for his treatment towards Draupadi. So they always sought ways and means to get back their kingdom.

Within a short time the Pandavas moved on to another forest. Meantime, Yudhishtira felt that the only way they could get back their kingdom was to wage a war with Duryodhana. For this purpose they had to secure necessary weapons and collect an ar my for which they had to contact kings friendly to them.

Wicked people always remain wicked. They take great delight in harassing good people. Duryodhana after banishing the Pandavas was afraid that they would reclaim their kingdom once

their exile was over. That is why he wanted to have them killed during the exile itself. Hence he counselled with Shakuni and Karna who were close to him and said, "Pandavas should now be weak without proper food and without proper weapons. It will be so easy to defeat them now". Shakuni and Karna agreed that it could be so. But, they needed the permission of the elders to put this plan into action. So, Duryodhana thought of an idea. Under the pretext of counting the cattlehead he invaded various woods and forests. When he entered the forest where Pandavas had sought refuge, Chitrasena, a Gandharva king, under instructions from Indra, waylaid Duryodhana and his army and defeated him. Shakuni and Karna fled from the place while Chitrasena dragged Duryodhana to Yudhishtira. Yudhishtira was a very righteous man. He always looked upon Duryodhana as one of his brothers. So, he ordered Duryodhana's release. Feeling insulted at his failure, Duryodhana returned to Hastinapur nursing his wounds and waiting for the right time to avenge defeat on the Pandavas.

During their exile in the forest, the Pandavas met several sages and always sought the righteous path from them. While in exile, Bhima met his elder brother Hanuman. Arjun observed penance

in the Himalayas and pleased with him, Eshwar, Yama, Kubera, Varuna and others granted him several very powerful weapons. Arjun also learnt dance and music from Chitrasena.

The exile period of the Pandavas was drawing to a close. One day a Brahmin came running to Yudhishtira and requested him to get him back the deer skin which had got entangled in a deer's horn. The Pandavas went in search of the deer but found it difficult to catch it. They were feeling thirsty after the chase and hence Yudhishtira asked his younger brother Sahadev to fetch water from any nearby lake.

Sahadeva did not return even after a long time. The worried Yudhishtira sent Nakul after him. Nakul also did not return. Then he sent Arjuna. But he too didn't return. Bhima also followed suit. So, Yudhishtira himself went in search of his brothers. After walking through a long distance, he saw a crystal clear lake. Lotus flowers had bloomed beautifully in the lake and presented a delightful scene. So, he thought that his brothers would be somewhere around, admiring the scenery. But when he looked around, he was shocked to see his very dear brothers dead by the banks of the lake. Yudhishtira could not believe his own eyes. How could

this have happened, he wondered. Tears welled up in his eyes at the thought that all his brothers were no longer alive. Actually, when the brothers went one by one to fetch water from the lake, an Yaksha had laid a condition that they could not touch water till they could answer his questions. But the thirsty brothers ignored him, drank the water and fell unconscious. Yudhishtira was not aware of this. He too could not contain his thirst. When he approached the lake to drink water, he heard an oracle. It belonged to this Yaksha.

"Answer my questions before drinking water", said the voice.

Without losing his cool Yudhishtira replied, "You can ask me anything you want, I will answer them to the best of my ability."

"Which has the fastest speed?"

"Speed of the mind"

"What is superior to earth?"

"Mother"

"What gives happiness to man?"

"To give up anger."

"How can one be the richest?"

"By giving up desire."

"What causes man's destruction?"

"His haughtiness".

"What weapon do you need to face danger?"

"Bravery"

The Yaksha had many more such questions to ask and when Yudhishtira answered them promptly he was highly pleased.

"I can make one of your brothers alive, but who should it be?" said the Yaksha. Yudhishtira loved all his brothers equally. But without hesitation he said, "My brother Nakul." Yaksha was surprised. "Instead of Bhima or Arjun, why do you ask for Nakul's life."

Yudhishtira said in a calm voice "Sir, I agree that Bhima and Arjun are my brothers. Nakul is my step mother Madri's son. I cannot sacrifice him for the sake of my own brothers".

Appreciating Yudhishtira's attitude the Yaksha brought back Nakula to life. "I will put back life to another brother of yours. Who should it be," he asked. Yudhishtira asked for Sahadev. Astonished, the Yaksha said, "Yudhishtira, at least now you could have asked for one of your valiant brothers." Yudhishtira had an apt reply, "Sir, when my father died, my mother Madri also gave up her life. But she ordained me to look after Nakul and Sahadev as my own children. How could I fail her?"

Extremely pleased with Yudhishtira the Yaksha brought back Bhima and Arjun also back to life and blessed all of them well. The Yaksha was none other than Yama, father of Yudhishtira. He blessed his own son by saying, "Your exile ends now. One more year incognito and your hardships will be over. So, you go to Matsya Kingdom and live there in disguise under King Virata".

The Pandavas along with Draupadi began their journey to Matsya Kingdom.

THE SLAYING OF KICHAKA

As per the condition laid down during the wager, the Pandavas completed twelve years of exile in the forest. They now had to live incognito for one year. During the year if their true identity was to be found out, they were to spend another twelve years in exile.

The Pandavas followed the Yaksha's instructions and entered the city of Matsya in disguise. Prior to that, they wrapped all their weapons in a gunny bag and hung it to a branch of a tree in a crematorium which was outside the city. Yudhishtira secured the friendship of king Virata under the name of Kankabhatta. Bhima was employed as a cook in the royal kitchen and was known as Valala. Arjun, who had learnt the art of dance and music under Chitrasena, called himself as Brihannala, and dressing up like a woman taught these arts to

the king's children. Sahadev obtained employment in the cowshed and Nakul in the stables. Draupadi worked as a maid to the queen under the name of Sairandri. It grieved Yudhishtira that all of them had to do menial tasks, especially Draupadi.

The queen had a brother called Kichaka. He was the commander-in-chief of Virata and wielded a lot of power and influence.

Once Kichaka went to the queen's chamber to meet his sister and saw Draupadi there. Draupadi was extremely beautiful and Kichaka was so smitten by her beauty that he talked indecently to her. Scared of his intentions, Draupadi escaped from his clutches and fled to her own room.

Kichaka who had great influence over his sister, went to her and told her about his passion for the maid. "Dear brother" Sudeshna, the queen, advised him, "Do not force any woman into submission. Give up your desire for her". But Kichaka would not listen. He persuaded his sister by saying, "After all, she is just a maid. Make her come to my chamber." Out of her love for her brother, the queen decided upon a plan.

That evening Sudeshna summoned Draupadi and instructed her to carry a jug of intoxicating drink to Kichaka. Draupadi hesitated but she had to follow the queen's orders. She went to the royal quarters of Kichaka and left the wine jug at the doorstep. She then hurriedly tried to get away from the place but Kichaka chased her. Trembling like a leaf, Draupadi fled to the court of Virata, fell at the feet of Yudhishtira who was in the midst of a game with the king, and begged him to come to her rescue. By that time, Kichaka reached the court and kicked her in the presence of all. Though Yudhishtira was pained to see this, he did not utter a single word, for he could not possibly reveal his relationship with Sairandri (Draupadi) and suffer another twelve years of exile. So he kept quiet. Crying over her helplessness Draupadi returned to her room. That very night she went to the royal kitchen, woke up Bhima and told him about Kichaka. "Either you kill Kichaka, or I will kill myself" threatened Draupadi in desperation. The enraged Bhima assured Draupadi that he would kill Kichaka. But not wanting to act in haste and reveal his true identity, Bhima advised Draupadi to entice Kichaka to the dancing hall the next night and that he would take care of the rest.

Draupadi visited Kichaka the next morning and pretending to yield to his desires, invited him to come alone to the dancing hall that night. The excited Kichaka waited for nightfall.

That night, Kichaka drank plenty of wine, dressed himself well and went to the dancing hall. In the dim light, he saw someone lying on a cot with a saree covered over the face. Thinking that this was Sairandri, he gently laid his hands on that form. Bhima who was on the cot draped in a saree, leapt upon Kichaka like a thunder, thrashed him into a lump and killed him. He then quietly slipped out of the hall and went to sleep on the kitchen floor.

In the morning, the news about Kichaka's death spread like fire all over the city; Sudeshna was filled with grief about her brother's death. She suspected Sairandri about this but had no proof.

The people of Virata were stunned that the valiant Kichaka met with such a terrible death. They felt that the person who killed Kichaka ought to be much more powerful than Kichaka himself. But none had the tiniest inkling that it was Bhima who killed Kichaka.

TO THE DEFENSE OF VIRATA

When Duryodhana heard about the mysterious way in which Kichaka was killed, he guessed that Bhima could have killed Kichaka, because it was a well known fact that only Bhima was as strong as Kichaka. So, Duryodhana surmised that the Pandavas were living under a different identity in the kingdom of Matsya. Moreover, word had reached Duryodhana that Sudeshna had a maid Sairandri who claimed that she had five Gandharvas as her husbands. There was no further doubt about the Pandavas being in the kingdom of Matsya.

'Kichaka's death will have weakened the Virata king. If we were to attack him now and if the Pandavas are really hiding there, they will definitely come out to fight to repay for his hospitality. We will thus have tracked them down and can banish them to the forest again thus thought Duryodhana. When he put forward this idea to Karna and others, they too agreed. Susharma, king of Trigarth was Duryodhana's friend and hence he agreed to invade Matsya by seizing the cattle and by destroying the gardens and fields on the way. Duryodhana was to launch his attack from the northern side.

Virata was yet to get over the loss of Kichaka and hence he was in no condition to face a war with the neighbouring kingdom. When he discussed his plight with Kanka, that is Yudhishtira, the latter said, "O King!, there is no time to waste. You summon the army and I will help you out. Similarly Valala, the cook, Dharmagranthi in the stable and Tantripala were earlier employed in the army of the Pandavas and so, given an opportunity, they will prove their skill in warfare." Virata was too glad to have help.

Bhima, Nakul and Sahadev were happy to prove their worth and in no time at all, defeated Susharma's army. Virata was delighted with the victory

Meanwhile, the Kauravas had rounded up the cows in the north and the cowherds ran to the palace to seek help. In the absence of Virata, they met Uttara Kumar, his son. Uttara boasted to them about his valour and also that he could defeat the Kauravas and recover the cows single-handed if only he could get a charioteer to take him to the battlefield. Sairandri who overheard this conversation suggested to him, "O Prince! Take Brihannala with you. She will be a very good charioteer".

Uttarkumar doubted whether a female could be a charioteer but since he did not have the courage to go alone, he agreed to the suggestion and took Brihannala (Arjun in disguise) to the warfront. But there, the sight of a big army, the sight of the wounded soldiers and the sound of clashing weapons unnerved the prince. Trembling with fear, he wanted to go back to the safety of his palace. But Arjun, in the disguise of Brihannala, encouraged Uttarkumar to fight like a brave person. "You have to fight to protect your land," he told the prince, "Otherwise, the enemy will destroy all of us. Do not fear I am with you."

Arjun took Uttarkumar to the tree in the crematorium where the Pandavas had hid their weapons. He asked the prince to bring down the weapons from the tree, which, he said, belonged to the Pandavas. The prince who no longer felt any cowardice, brought down the gleaming weapons from the tree. He felt that Brihannala was no ordinary person. He wanted to know her true identity. When Brihannala told him that she was Arjun, Uttara folded his hands in reverence. "Please forgive me for treating you a valiant hero, as a charioteer," he said in a humble tone. Arjun advised him about behaving like a warrior and together they hastened towards the battlefield.

When Duryodhana saw Uttarkumar approaching the battlefield with a female charioteer, he felt that victory was undoubtedly very easy. Arjun observed from a distance Bhishma, Drona and Kripacharya standing along with Karna and Duryodhana in the battlefield. He stringed his bow and used three arrows. One arrow fell at the feet of Bhishma, the other at Drona's and the third at Kripa's feet. This salutation made all of them exclaim, "Arjun is here". On hearing this, Duryodhana immediately cried aloud, "Arjun has been identified before the

exile period is over. The Pandavas should undergo twelve more years of exile." But Drona clarified and said, "The stipulated period ended just before we recognised Arjun as the charioteer."

There was an argument over this between Drona, Duryodhana and Drona's son Ashwathama. Finally Bhishma put an end to this war of words by reminding them that they had to urgently confront Arjun.

Arjun and Uttarkumar fought valiantly and defeated the Kaurava army. Duryodhana fled from the battlefield leaving behind the stolen cattle. The entire army retreated to Hastinapur.

Virata who was overjoyed to hear about this victory against the Kauravas arranged a grand welcome to his son, Uttar. But he did not realise that a youngster like Uttar could not have defeated war veterans like Bhishma and Drona. He was so full of praise for his son. So, when Yudhishtira revealed the truth that Brihannala was the true reason for winning the war, Virata was annoyed that Kanka equated Uttar with a mere woman. In a fit of anger, Virata flung the dice he was playing on Kanka's face. Kanka was hurt and blood oozed from his face. Immediately Sairandri hastened to his side, wiped the blood with a cloth

and squeezed it into a cup. Virata was further enraged. He shouted at Sairandri, "Why are you concerned about a total stranger?" he asked her.

"Kanka is not his true name" replied Sairandri. "He is a king and it does not augur well for your kingdom if his blood drops on the floor." Virata was very confused with this reply.

Right at that moment, Uttarkumar entered the palace and revealed to his father, the identity of Brihannala, Kanka, Sairandri, Bhima, Nakul and Sahadev. Virata was aghast at the thought that he had treated the mighty Pandavas as servants and that Draupadi worked as a maid to the queen. The queen sought Draupadi's forgiveness.

Virata, in gratitude to the Pandavas for defending the kingdom, gave his daughter, Princess Uttara, in marriage to Arjun's son Abhimanyu in the presence of Krishna, Balaram and Drupada.

The exile and the incognito life of the Pandavas came to an end. What would be their next action was the thought foremost in everybody's mind. Some suggested to the Pandavas to defeat the Kauravas through a war and win back their kingdom. But war meant bloodshed and loss of lives. Hence Krishna advised the Pandavas to avoid a war. "But don't be cowards", he counselled, "If a peaceful settlement between you and the Kauravas cannot be reached, let us wage a war. But before that, let us try to reach a compromise with them." Krishna wanted to avoid war, though he knew that Duryodhana would never listen to any reason. Krishna knew that a war was inevitable between the Pandavas and the Kauravas.

KRISHNA'S MEDIATION

Duryodhana was a very adamant person. He could never concede anything at all. The messenger sent by the Pandavas through Drupada, read out before Duryodhana his various misdeeds against the Pandavas and called upon him to return their kingdom. The messenger also warned Duryodhana of the consequences of war if he did not agree for a peaceful settlement. Duryodhana was enraged to receive such a message. The elderly Bhishma who was present in the court advised Duryodhana to honourably give back Pandava's share of the kingdom. Otherwise the Kauravas would all be destroyed, he warned. Karna scorned Bhishma for siding the Pandavas. "They have foolishly lost their kingdom. Why should we return it?" was his argument. Dhrithrashtra sent an appeal to the Pandavas through Sanjay that they should give up their claim over the kingdom and avert a war. Pandavas were temporarily staying near Virata city of Matsya land. When Sanjay tried to convince Yudhishtira to give up any claim over the kingdom, Yudhishtira politely refused. "I have been made a king once and hence cannot live like a beggar. We Pandavas are not greedy. We are only asking for our share of the kingdom. If Duryodhana opposes this, at least give us five villages, one for each of us. We shall be content with this offer and shall not wage a war" he said.

When Sanjay conveyed this message to Dhrithrashtra and his sons, Duryodhana laughed. The mighty Pandavas, with all their talk of dignity, asking for a mere five villages amused him. But his father found sense in this and told him, "Son! I am sure you can give away the five villages. The rest of the empire will be yours. Duryodhana flatly refused by saying, "Dear father, I shall not part with even a needle-point of land" and walked out of the meeting.

Duryodhana just did not want to listen to any good advice or to reason. He was obsessed with destroying the Pandavas totally. Karna, Shakuni, Duhshyasana and others encouraged him in this. Elders like Bhishma, Drona and Kripa were totally ignored. The blind Dhrithrashtra was like a puppet in his son's hands.

Duryodhana's proclamation that he would not give even a needle-point of land to the Pandavas dismayed Krishna. He felt that there was no more scope for peace talks but as a final effort, decided to personally go to Hastinapur and negotiate with the Kauravas. Draupadi did not favour this. The wicked ones ought to be punished was her attitude. She told her five husbands, "if you do not want to wage a war, I will seek the help of my father, the king Drupada and Dhrishtadyumna, my brother. I have five sons to go to the battlefield." She could not forget the utter humiliation she faced at the hands of the Kauravas at a full gathering. Krishna consoled her by saying, "Dear sister, Duryodhana will never agree to a peaceful settlement and hence the final outcome will be a war. But I will have to make a last attempt." So saying, he departed for Hastinapur.

Duryodhana wanted to accord a grand welcome to Krishna. But instead of going straight to the court of the Kauravas, Krishna spent some time at Vidur's house and then went to the court, where Bhishma, Drona, Dhrithrashtra and Vidura were present. Duryodhana warmly welcomed Krishna and offered him a jewel studded throne. "Krishna, it was below your dignity to stay with low-born Vidura. You should have accepted my hospitality," chided Duryodhana. Vidura, hurt by Duryodhana's cruel words refused to co-operate

with him any further. Duryodhana at that moment, did not realise what a loss this would be.

Krishna rose from his seat and facing the king, explained his intention to avert a war between the Kauravas and the Pandavas. "Dhrithrashtra, please treat the Pandavas honourably and return their share of the kingdom. Do not cause destruction to the Kuru clan", Krishna said.

Dhrithrashtra pleaded his helplessness and so Krishna turned his attention towards Duryodhana and said gently, "Duryodhana, please be reasonable. If not half the kingdom, at least five villages will make the Pandavas happy." Duryodhana stuck to his word, said a firm 'No' and walked out of the court.

Krishna pleaded with the elders about the senseless attitude of Duryodhana. "It is better to do away with one Duryodhana to save the other Kauravas" was Krishna's better advice to the others.

"Krishna on the pretence of mediation is plotting to kill me," accused Duryodhana when he heard about this advice. He immediately ordered his brother Duhshyasana to seize Krishna with ropes.

How is it possible to tie down the Protector of the Universe, the Omnipotent Krishna? When Duryodhana and his brothers rushed back to the palace court to imprison Krishna, Krishna revealed his Viswarupa. Wherever Duryodhana and Duhshyasana turned, they saw only Krishna. The courtiers looked like Krishna; There was Krishna on every seat and on every throne. Who was the real Krishna?

Krishna's Viswarupa was the magnificent revelation of the Supreme Being. Even the blind Dhrithrashtra temporarily regained his eyesight and was able to see the Vishwarupa. While all the others were stupefied by this revelation, the ignorant Duryodhana termed it as a magic trick of Krishna. When Duryodhana reiterated his obstinacy, Krishna left the court after resuming his normal form.

He went straight to Kunthi and told her about the events of the day. She was extremely distressed to learn that her sons had to resort to war. When she thought of Karna, her heart felt heavy. She wanted to reveal the secret about Karna's birth in the hope that once he learnt the truth, he would not fight against his own brothers.

Krishna also agreed with her, but suggested that she should make Karna promise her that he would not use the same arrow twice in the war.

Mother and son were to come face to face at last!

Kunthi knew that Karna offered his prayers to the Sun God every morning by the side of the river. So she waited for him till his prayers were over. When he turned back, he saw Kunthi. He touched her feet in reverence. In a trembling voice, Kunthi addressed Karna as 'Son". Karna felt that she wanted to say something important to him.

"Son, you have always believed yourself to be Adiratha's son. This is not the truth. You were born a Kshatriya and you were born to me." So saying, she could no longer control her emotions and wept bitterly. She then told him about his birth and about setting him afloat in the river. She wanted to be forgiven for her action.

On hearing the truth about his birth Karna said sadly "Mother, you have got me into a predicament by revealing the truth. I can only say that fate has been very cruel to me."

Kunthi touched him gently and continued to say, "Child! You are my eldest born. The Pandavas are your younger brothers. Not knowing the truth, you have joined hands with Duryodhana. But it is never too late. Come back to us and be a king. I assure you that you will have the abiding loyalty of your younger brothers."

Karna was a true friend of Duryodhana. He was ever grateful to his friend for his large-heartedness in crowning him as the king of Anga. So he told Kunthi in a firm voice, "Mother! I cannot give up my friendship for the sake of a throne. Duryodhana has total confidence in me. I cannot betray him at this moment."

"Son! You have no consideration for your poor mother", asked Kunthi. Though Karna did not offer any reply, he could not forget the humiliation he had suffered in his entire life as being the son of a charioteer. Neither Kunthi nor the Pandavas could wipe out his unpleasant memories.

"Please forgive me", said Karna to Kunthi, "I promise you that I shall not fight against Yudhishtira, Bhima, Nakul or Sahadev. But I shall not spare Arjun. I will not hesitate even to kill him. If he were to die at my hands, you still will have five sons. If I were to be killed by Arjun, you will still have five sons."

Kunthi then took courage and told Karna, "Son! You speak like a true Kshatriya. But promise me that you shall not use the same arrow twice on Arjun." The ever-generous Karna agreed to this and Kunthi returned home with a heavy heart.

Karna walked towards the palace with mixed emotions.

Such is the path of destiny!

THE KURUKSHETRA WAR

There was no doubt in everybody's mind that war was inevitable. Many people felt that cousins ought not resort to war, fighting over land. Others were of the opinion that Duryodhana ought not have been so adamant. The fact that Lord Krishna had himself tried to mediate between the hostile cousins and had failed disillusioned many. When Krishna returned from Hastinapur and informed Yudhishtira about the outcome of his trip, he felt very sad. The peace loving Yudhishtira lamented that bloodshed could not be stopped. Krishna returned to Dwaraka.

Drupada and Krishna were the only friends the Pandavas had. Drupad was waiting for an opportunity to avenge his daughter's humiliation. He was ready to lend his army to Dharmaraja. Krishna's army consisted of Yadavas. Duryodhana wanted to avail of this army's services. Moreover he knew that Krishna's support was of utmost importance. So he went to Dwaraka to meet Krishna. Meanwhile, Arjun also reached Dwaraka to seek Krishna's help for Yudhishtira. Krishna who knew of their intentions, pretended to be fast asleep as soon as

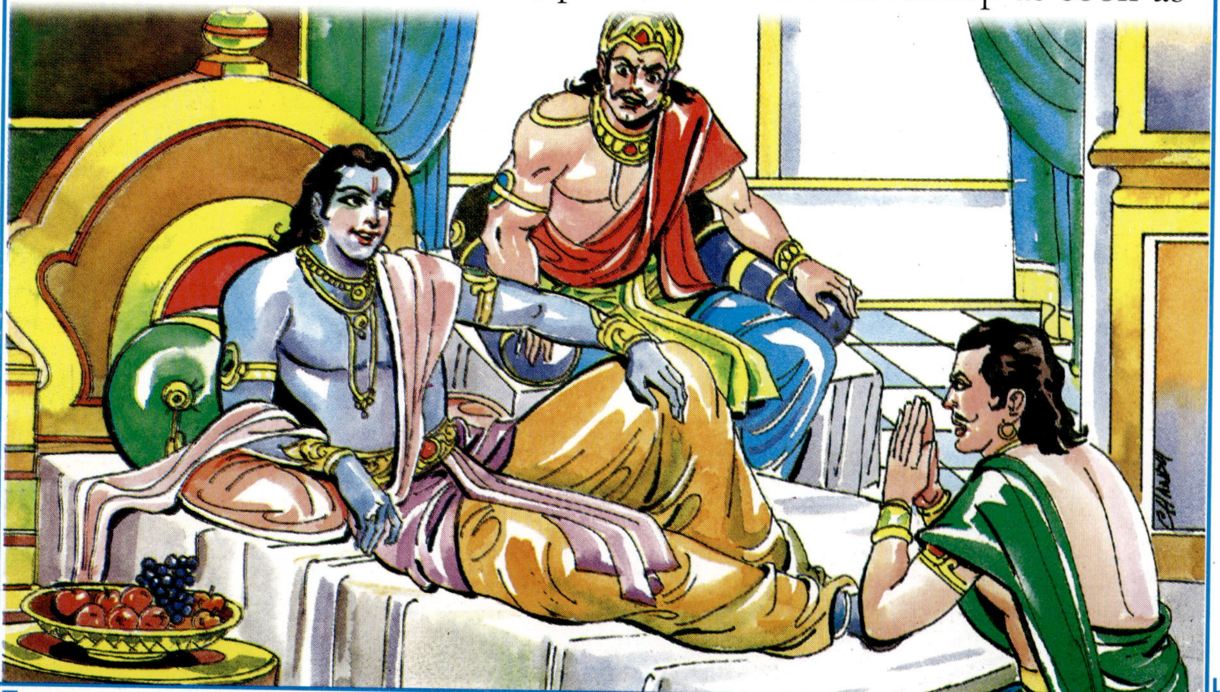

Duryodhana and Arjun reached his doorstep. Duryodhana, befitting the status of a king, preferred to sit on the seat placed near Krishna's head. He waited for Krishna to wake up. Arjun sat on a stool near Krishna's feet. As soon as Krishna opened his eyes, he saw Arjun first. Naturally, he could not have noticed Duryodhana first as he was sitting near the head. And naturally, Krishna talked to Arjun first. Duryodhana could not tolerate this and so he emitted a sound to catch Krishna's attention. Immediately Krishna turned towards him and exclaimed, "Oh Duryodhana! You are also here. This is an honour for me. What can I do for you?"

Duryodhana replied, "Yashodanandan, I have come to seek your help in the forthcoming war. Undoubtedly, victory will be mine. Hence, please be with us." Arjun also said "Krishna, I am also here to ask for your help. We will be honoured to have you with us."

Krishna was in a dilemma. Both of them were his relatives and hence he ought to extend help to both of them. So he told them, "Dear Duryodhan and dear Arjun, both of you are my relatives. If I come to your help, my army will also assist you. But I will not personally take up arms. Nor will I participate in the actual fighting. So you have an option. One of you can take my entire army and the other could have me. But since I spoke to Arjun first, he will have the first privilege,"

The Pandavas were aware of Krishna's divinity. So Arjun at once said, "Krishna, I do not want your army. We want only you with us." Duryodhana was relieved to hear this. After all, Krishna had already said that he himself would not fight. So, what was the use of having him? He cried out in delight, "Krishna, in that case, give me your army." Krishna agreed to both these requests.

The war fever gripped one and all. The Pandavas and the Kauravas reviewed their respective armies to assess their strength. Duryodhana had a sister by name Dushyale. Her husband was Jayadrata, the Saindhava king. So, Duryodhana had his backing. Shalya, the king of Madra also was with the Kauravas. Susharma, the king of Trigarth and

his children had always extended their help to Duryodhana. The Yadava army sent by Krishna also swelled Duryodhana's strength. Bhishma, Drona, Kripa, Ashwathama were already with the Kauravas. Thus, the Kaurava's army numbered eleven Akshohinis*

The Pandavas had the support of Drupada, Dhrishtadyumna, Amba who was born as Shikandi to Drupada in order to settle scores with Bhishma, Virata, Satyaki and others. Bhima and Arjun, themselves were very valiant. Abhimanyu, the fourteen year old son of Arjun and Subhadra also announced that he was taking part in the war. Bhima's son Ghatotkacha was also there. The Pandavas in all, had seven Akshohinis. Yudhishtira divided these into seven divisions and appointed a commander-in-chief for each one of them. Bhima headed one such division. Since Krishna did not wish to participate in the war, he told Arjun that he would be his charioteer.

One Akshohini = A battalion consisting of 21,870 elephants, 21,870 Chariots; 65,6I0 horses and an infantry of 1,09,350.

Duryodhana also made hectic preparations to appoint commanders-in-chief for his army. The elderly Bhishma, a great warrior, was appointed as the Supreme General in charge over all the other chiefs. Karna, who always felt that Bhishma had a soft corner for the Pandavas, was annoyed by this appointment. He wanted the post for himself. He therefore refused to take up arms till Bhishma continued as the Supreme General. This infighting saddened Duryodhana. But he could not snatch away the post from a person of Bhishma's stature.

Bhishma, the father figure of the Kuru clan announced the commencement of the Kurukshetra war.

The Kaurava army and the Pandava army faced each other in the battlefield of Kurukshetra.

Sri Krishna entered the battlefield as Arjun's charioteer. The Hanumadhwaja (flag showing Hanuman) fluttered atop the chariot. Krishna blew the Panchajanya conch and Arjun blew the Devadatta conch to indicate the starting of war.

The beating of war-drums, the neighing of the horses and the trumpeting sound of the elephants filled Arjun with the excitement of war. But as he neared the Kaurava army, he saw the grand old man Bhishma, he saw his Gurus Drona and Kripa and he saw his cousins and other relatives. All of them were dear to him. All of them were the revered ones.

Arjun hesitatingly asked Krishna, "Should I kill my own kith and kin for my selfishness? Should I kill my own friends just to gain victory over them? I am unable to do it." So saying he quickly put down his weapons.

To remove this deep agitation in Arjun's mind, Krishna spoke to him softly, "Arjun, war is inevitable. This may seem to be a cruel, unjust way to you. But have you forgotten the grave injustice meted out by the Kauravas? Such a conflict arises between humanbeings upon this world. Who are you to kill? Who are they to be killed? It is God's will. We are only empowered to carry out our duties assigned to each of us."

Krishna further explained the various means of attaining God. He preached Arjun about the path of devotion and the path of duty. To fight for justice is duty. "Do your duty without desiring for reward or for fame" was the gospel of Sri Krishna. This is known as the **Bhagavad Gita,** hailed as the treasure of knowledge for the entire mankind.

Lord Krishna then exhibited his Viswarupa and said "I am the beginning and the end of all beings upon this world. I am Omnipresent and Omnipotent. Without my being, nothing lives. I am present in the plant, in the tree, in the atmosphere, in the sky and everything else upon the earth. I protect those who believe in me. O Arjun! Hence give up the doubts that haunt you, pick up the weapons and fight."

Listening to the Gitopadesha (Preaching of Gita), a new light of knowledge dawned upon Arjun. 'The Supreme Being is the puppeteer and we are mere puppets in His hands. It is now my duty to fight and this is the path of duty' - thus Arjun readied himself for the war.

The Kurukshetra war was waged for eighteen days. During these days, a lot of blood was shed. Each day witnessed the death of thousands of soldiers, horses and elephants. From dawn to dusk, the war went on. It provided ample opportunity to the soldiers and to the commanders to prove their worth. Every evening at sunset, a bugle was blown to indicate the end of the day's battle. And each night, the losses in terms of men and animals were reviewed and the next day's plan of action finalised.

Bhishma alone waged the war for ten days. Abhimanyu faced Bhishma the first day of the war but had to concede defeat at the hands of Bhishma. Virata's children who came to the help of Abhimanyu were killed.

Arjun would make up his mind each day that he would kill Bhishma but did not have the heart to kill the grand old man who was a father-figure to all of them. Bhishma's attacks were so devastating that it looked as if a ball of fire was engulfing the enemies. Because of Bhishma, the death toll in the Pandava camp was very high. Hence Krishna often urged Arjun to kill Bhishma but seeing Arjun's hesitancy in doing so, on the ninth day of the war, Krishna jumped out of the chariot with the intention of fighting with Bhishma. But Arjun reminded him about his decision on not taking part in the war directly. Arjun promised Krishna that Bhishma would be slain the next day.

It was neither easy nor possible to kill Bhishma. The tenth day of the Kurukshetra war dawned. At the instance of Krishna, Arjun made Shikandi, the son of Drupada stand in front of him. He then attacked Bhishma upon which, Bhishma did not wish to fight against a man who was a woman in previous birth and decided to lay down his weapons. As he could command his own death, he also decided to welcome death. So he purposely did not retaliate against Arjun's arrows. With arrows sticking all over his body, Bhishma Pitamah fell down. But his body could not touch the ground because of the numerous arrows sticking out. It was thus a bed of arrows for Bhishma.

The battlefield suddenly was quiet. A cease fire was announced. The Pandavas and the Kauravas rushed to the side of Bhishma. Duryodhana tried to place a pillow under Bhishma's head but the great man refused. He wanted a pillow befitting a warrior. Arjun understood what he meant and created a support for Bhishma's head by striking three arrows on the ground and under the head. Even at that moment, Bhishma advised Duryodhana to make peace with the Pandavas. But Duryodhana refused yet again.

Bhishma felt very thirsty. At once Arjun shot an arrow into the earth. Pure water gushed out from the hole and like a fountain, reached Bhishma's lips gently. It looked as if Bhishma's mother Ganga had surfaced from the ground to bid farewell to her noble son. Bhishma then said, "I will lie here till the sun travels northwards. My soul will then depart." His body thus lay in the battlefield. The day's fighting was over.

Duryodhana returned to his camp to decide upon the next Supreme Commander in the place of Bhishma. The loss of Bhishma was a great setback to Duryodhana.

Karna was appointed the Supreme Commander for the eleventh day of the war. But Karna, out of respect for Drona, gave up the position in his favour. The eleventh day of the war dawned. Bugles were sounded and conches were blown. Duryodhana had instructed Drona that he should imprison Yudhishtira as the day's trophy. He intended to banish the Pandavas to the forest forever. Drona reluctantly agreed to this task as he felt obligated to the Kauravas.

When Drona launched a direct attack on Yudhishtira, Arjun tried to move closer to his brother but was stopped by Susharma's children who also fought bravely. Like a ray of lightning, Arjun was at the side of Yudhishtira one moment and the next moment was fighting against Susharma's children, the Samsaptakas. On the twelfth day, Drona planned to capture Yudhishtira by engaging Arjun in a fight with the Samsaptakas but in a swift move, Arjun rescued his elder brother. That night, Duryodhana admonished the elderly Drona for his failure to prevent Arjun from rescuing his brother.

Dronacharya was very much hurt by these words. This made him all the more determined to seize Dharmaraya and to gain victory for the Kauravas. He therefore rearranged his army around Yudhishtira so that he could be easily captured while Arjun would be busy fighting against the Samsaptakas. This formation was called Chakravyuh, an extremely difficult maze and only Krishna, Arjun and his young son Abhimanyu knew how to break the maze. But Abhimanyu only knew how to get in.

Since Arjun and Krishna were away from the spot, the responsibility of penetrating the maze fell upon the young but valiant shoulders of Abhimanyu. He therefore told his uncle that they were to follow him. Yudhishtira at first hesitated but since there was no other option, he agreed.

With the blessings of his uncle, Abhimanyu drove his chariot and penetrated the maze. But the Pandavas were prevented from following Abhimanyu by Jayadrat, the son of Sindhuraj. As a result, Abhimanyu was surrounded by enemies. He fought alone but could not withstand the attack for very long. Duhshyasan cut Abhimanyu's limbs one by one. Karna pierced the boy's body with his arrows. Jayadrat drove his spear through the inert body and finally killed him. The entire ground was covered with Abhimanyu's blood and the sun also set, as if unable to witness the scene.

The Kaurava camp was overjoyed with Abhimanyu's death and on the other hand, the Pandava army was plunged into sorrow. Arjun who returned to the camp after defeating the Samsaptakas was met with mourning and immense grief. When he heard about the way in which his dearest son was killed, he swore, "Before the sun sets tomorrow, I shall kill Jayadrata who was the cause of my son's death." In his grief, Arjun also accused Yudhishtira and Bhima of being irresponsible and having sent a youngster like Abhimanyu to penetrate the Chakravyuh. He could not console his wife Subhadra and Uttara, Abhimanyu's wife.

News of Arjun's vow reached the Kauravas. Duryodhana was very eager to protect Jayadrata against Arjun by waging the war himself till the evening. There was a severe fight between the two stalwarts - Arjun and Duryodhana and none could gain an upper-hand. The day was drawing to an end. Duryodhana thought that since Arjun could not keep up his vow to kill Jayadrat the same evening, he (Arjun) would, out of shame, commit suicide. And victory would be Duryodhana's. To meet the situation, Krishna covered the rays of the sun with his hand and made it look as if the sun had set. Jayadrata feeling confident that he had survived the day

emerged out of his hiding and on Krishna's instructions, Arjuna hit Jayadrata with his bow chopping off his head.

The war was continued even at night and when Bhima killed seven of Duryodhana's brothers, in retaliation, Karna used his Shaktya weapon on Ghatotkacha, Bhima's son and beheaded him. Ghatotkacha was the second son to die for the Pandavas.

When the war raged on for the fifteenth consecutive day, Krishna expressed his opinion that unless and until Drona was killed the Pandavas would never be victorious. Hence he suggested to Arjun, "Arjun, shout loudly in the midst of the fighting that Drona's son Aswatthama has been killed. The grief striken Drona will lose all his enthusiasm to fight and thus it will be easy for us to defeat him." Arjun did not like this idea of deceiving his Guru. Krishna then put forward this idea to Bhima. Bhima killed an elephant by name Aswatthama and cried out aloud that Aswatthama died. When Drona heard this, he at once knew that this was Krishna's trick. He therefore announced that he would believe his son to be dead only if the ever truthful Yudhishtira were to say it. So, at the instance of Krishna, Yudhishtira called out "Aswatthama Hatha Kunjarah" (Aswatthama, the elephant, has been killed). Just as he was saying it, Krishna blew the conch so loud that

Drona only heard that Aswatthama had been killed. Since Yudhishtira had uttered these words, Drona took it to be true, threw down his weapons and sat down on the ground. His beloved son's death had robbed him of the will to live. Seizing this opportunity, Dhrishtadyumna, in retaliation against Drona's humiliation of his father, drew out his sword and severed Drona's head.

On hearing the news about his father's death, Aswatthama went berserk and brandishing his sword, attacked the enemy and killed many soldiers. He swore that he would wipe out the entire Pandava race to avenge for his father's death.

Drona's death doubled Duryodhana's grief. He then installed Karna as the Supreme Commander. The war went on relentlessly with a great deal of death and destruction. There was intense fighting between Bhima and Duhshyasan. Recalling what Duhshyasan had done to Draupadi, Bhima's anger exploded like a volcano. He leapt upon Duhshyasan, lifted him up and using all his strength thrashed him down. Bhima then tore Duhshyasan's arm and sucked the blood from his body.

Dhrithrashtra was grief striken when he heard about the gory way in which his son was killed. But it was too late to stop the war.

The sixteenth day of the battle witnessed Karna and Arjun confront each other. Shalya was Karna's charioteer.

The battle between Karna and Arjun was a clash of epic proportions.

Determined to kill Arjun, Karna used an arrow, which was a deadly weapon spewing serpents. As it was about to strike Arjun, Krishna pushed the chariot down into the earth by a few inches. The arrow could only knock down Arjun's headgear. The arrow of serpents returned to Karna and wanted to be reused on Arjun. But Karna recalled the promise made to Kunthi that he would not use the same weapon twice. Arjun was thus saved.

As fate would have it, Karna's chariot got stuck in the blood soaked mud. His charioteer Shalya refused to get down and lift the chariot up. "Karna, you have so often boasted about your strength. Prove it now," he said in ridicule.

With no other alternative, Karna jumped out of the chariot and tried to lift the chariot single-handed. Arjun took advantage of the situation and poured a rain of arrows on Karna. "Please do not take undue

advantage of me, O Arjun!" cried out Karna, "Have you forgotten the code of conduct that you cannot attack an unarmed man?" Red in face, Arjun hurriedly put down his quiver full of arrows. But Krishna laughed scornfully and said "Yes, Arjun, have you forgotten that Karna was among those who hacked Abhimanyu to death? What was Karna doing when Dushyasana was trying to disrobe Draupadi, a defenceless woman in front of everybody? Just don't waste your time. Don't lose this chance. Shoot your arrows at Karna."

Arjun saw wisdom in Krishna's advice. He therefore shot his arrows, one after the other, at Karna. Karna forgot all the mantras he had to utter before using any arrow.

Parashurama's curse was upon him. The generous Karna had already donated his armour and earrings to Indra. His strength had subsided. Since he had already used the Shaktya weapon to kill Ghatotkacha, he did not have a suitable weapon against Arjun. To add to his misfortune, the wheel of the chariot just did not budge.

Arjun used his most powerful arrow which instantly severed Karna's head. A glorious light emitted out of Karna's body and submerged into the Sun. The Sun God took away his valiant son. On witnessing this scene, Arjun realised that Karna was an extra-ordinary person. Instead of feeling happy, Arjun felt bereaved. He returned to his camp in a subdued mood.

Duryodhana grieved over his dearest friend's death for hours. None of the surviving Kauravas could console him. He felt that a terrible vacuum had been created in his army with the deaths of Drona and Karna. Seeing his anguish, Kripacharya tried to advise him, "Duryodhana, at least now make peace with the Pandavas. Survive this holocaust and enjoy the rest of your life." Even at that moment, Duryodhana turned a deaf ear to the advice. He appointed Shalya as the General with orders to fight till the very end.

Shalya fell a victim to Yudhishtira's arrow on the eighteent day of the battle. On the same day, the wicked Shakuni was kille

by Sahadev and the surviving brothers of Duryodhana by Bhima. Only Kripa, Aswatthama and Duryodhana were left.

At this stage, Duryodhana belatedly realised that he could not escape from the enemies. So he hid in a pool of water.

The Pandavas reached the spot shortly, and challenged him to come out of his hiding. When he emerged out of water, Duryodhana picked up his mace and fought with Bhima. Both of them were equal in strength and skill and the combat raged for a long time. Bhima who found it impossible to knock down Duryodhana looked at Krishna who made a sign by slapping the thighs. Bhima recalled the vow he had made when Duryodhana humiliated Draupadi. When the Pandavas had lost the game of dice, Duryodhana had called Draupadi his maid and had taunted her to sit on his lap. The enraged Bhima had vowed, "Duryodhana! I will kill you by breaking your thighs." Though such a method of killing an enemy was contrary to the rules of war, Bhima recalled the grave injustices meted out by Duryodhana and dealing a powerful blow with his mace he thrashed Duryodhana's thighs into a pulp. Howling with pain, Duryodhana fell down and Bhima kicked him hard on the head.

"Stop, Bhima", cried out his elder brother, "It is not right on your part to kick a king in the head." On hearing this, Duryodhana talking with great difficulty told his cousin, "Yudhishtira, you may have scored a victory over me. But don't forget that this is an unethical victory for you. Arjun hid himself behind a woman to defeat the great Bhishma. You uttered a lie to make Drona give up fighting. Karna was killed when he was unarmed. And now Bhima has broken the rules of the war and thrashed my thighs with a mace. After all these events, you have finally managed to call Bhima's act of kicking my head as Adharma (unethical). Let him do whatever he wants to. It will only belittle him. I am an emperor. I am not a coward. I shall die a brave death after waging the war. A valiant world is awaiting me. My kingdom is now yours. You have paid a heavy price to gain it. I am doubtful whether it will bring you peace of mind."

Yudhishtira was filled with sorrow at the thought that his cousin was to die shortly. Krishna was nonchalant. The Pandavas returned from the battlefield in a state of melancholy.

Duryodhana battled for his life. This was a tragic story created due to his own greed. Aswatthama who could not tolerate Duryodhana's condition vowed before him, "O Emperor! Do not think that you are the only one to hate the Pandavas. For, I cannot forgive them for their deception in killing my father, I shall avenge by beheading the Pandavas one by one." Duryodhana, even when he was in his deathbed, was delighted to hear this, "Go, Guruputr! I am appointing you as the General. Show me the dead bodies of the Pandavas before I die."

It was a dark and terrible night. Aswatthama came to know that the Pandavas were fast asleep in their camp. Actually instead of the Pandavas and Krishna, the Panchalas, that is, Draupadi's five sons and Dhristadyumna had chosen to sleep in the tent. Without even bothering to look at their faces, Aswatthama butchered all of them and hastened to Duryodhana's side. But by that time Duryodhana had already died.

In the morning Draupadi was inconsolable when she heard about the killing of her five sons. She went to Yudhishtira and told him that if Aswatthama was not killed, she would commit suicide on the funeral pyre of her children. The Pandavas went in search of him and found him hiding in a place near the river. When he saw them approaching, Aswatthama charged a blade of grass with a deadly mantra and threw it towards them. They avoided the blade of grass; but in order to wipe out their race, the manthric grass tried to hit the womb of Uttara who was pregnant with Abhimanyu's son. Lord Krishna at once stopped the grass blade with his hand and thus protected Uttara's womb. Frustrated by this, Aswatthama escaped to the forest. He was never to be seen again.

The battle of Kurukshetra was over but Yudhishtira did not find peace of mind in any way. While the entire Hastinapur mourned over the loss of their kith and kin killed in the war, Dhrithrashtra and Gandhari wept over the loss of their sons and Kunthi over Karna's death. The blind Dhrithrashtra had the misfortune of cremating his own children. But still he hated the Pandavas and especially Bhima. So, when the Pandavas came to him to pay their respects, Dhrithrashtra embraced them one by one, without there being any love or affection in those embraces. When he was about to embrace Bhima, the wise Krishna pushed Bhima aside and placed a metal statue before the blind king. The blind but very strong king hugged the statue so tightly that it was reduced to pieces. He thought Bhima was dead but when he learnt the truth, he suppressed his anger and blessed the Pandavas.

When Kunthi told her sons that Karna was her eldest born, the grief striken Yudhishtira performed the funeral ceremony for Karna. The Pandavas also performed the last rites for all the other departed souls and bathed in the Ganga to atone for their sins. Subsequently Krishna took Yudhishtira to Bhishma who was still alive. The grand old man gave his blessings for the coronation of Yudhishtira as the emperor of Hastinapur. He also advised the new emperor about the path of

Dharma. Shortly afterwards, when the sun was in the northernly direction, Bhishma invited death and breathed his last.

Yudhishtira ruled over Hastinapur well and his reign brought peace and prosperity to the citizens. The Pandavas looked after Dhrithrashtra and Gandhari with love, affection and respect. Yudhishtira even performed their last rites when they died. Krishna stayed in Dwaraka for thirty six years after the battle of Kurukshetra before he completed his avatar (incarnation).

These events created a detachment towards life among the Pandavas and Draupadi. They therefore crowned Parikshit, son of Abhimanyu as the emperor of Hastinapur and proceeded towards heaven. A dog followed them and kept them company all along. When they reached the gates of heaven, the dog was not allowed entry. So, Yudhishtira and the others did not want to get into heaven and preferred to go to Naraka, the hell.

The Devas were pleased with the Pandavas for their love towards the animal and let all of them into heaven.